EDGE
BOOKS ™

DRAW ASTONISHING WARRIOR MASH-UPS

BY MARI BOLTE
ART BY KAN-J

CAPSTONE PRESS
a capstone imprint

Edge Books are published by Capstone Press,
1710 Roe Crest Drive, North Mankato, Minnesota 56003
www.mycapstone.com

Library of Congress Cataloging-in-Publication Data
Names: Bolte, Mari, author.
Title: Draw astonishing warrior mash-ups / by Mari Bolte.
Description: North Mankato, Minnesota : Edge Books, Capstone
Press, 2018. |
  Series: Drawing mash-ups | Includes bibliographical references
and index.
  | Audience: Ages 9-15. | Audience: Grades 4 to 6.
Identifiers: LCCN 2017021450| ISBN 9781515769378 (library binding) |
ISBN 9781515769415 (ebook pdf)
Subjects: LCSH: Combat in art—Juvenile literature. | Fantasy in
art—Juvenile literature. | Drawing--Technique--Juvenile literature.
Classification: LCC NC1763.C58 B66 2018 | DDC 704.9/493554—dc23
LC record available at https://lccn.loc.gov/2017021450

Editorial Credits
Brann Garvey, designer; Kathy McColley, production specialist

Image Credits
Illustrations: Kan-J, except Capstone: Q2A Media, 31; Photos: Capstone
Studio: Karon Dubke, 5 (all); Backgrounds and design elements: Capstone

Printed and bound in the USA.
010364F17

TABLE OF CONTENTS

PEN VS. PAPER

Does your imagination fight for your attention? Drawing mash-ups throw two (or more!) unlikely combinations in the ring and make them battle it out. Use the ideas in the book, and then re-mash them for a new set of ideas! Challenge your friends to see who can draw the fiercest, scariest, or even funniest warriors.

MATERIALS

The artwork in this book was created digitally, but that doesn't mean your own art can't look equally amazing.

It all starts with a pencil and paper! Use light pencil strokes to shape your creation. Shading, hash marks, and curved lines can really make your mash-ups pop off the page.

When you're happy with how your sketches look, darken the pencil lines and erase any overlapping areas. Use a pen to outline and add shadows and detail.

Markers or colored pencils will truly bring your art to life. Experiment with shading, outlines, blending, or using different shades of the same color to make gradients. Or try out a new art supply! Chalk or watercolor pencils, oil crayons, or pastels could add an extra challenge.

BUG-EYED BOUNTY HUNTER

You can run, but you can't hide. This bounty hunter sees everything! Escape is impossible once he has you in his sights.

STEP 1

STEP 2

STEP 3

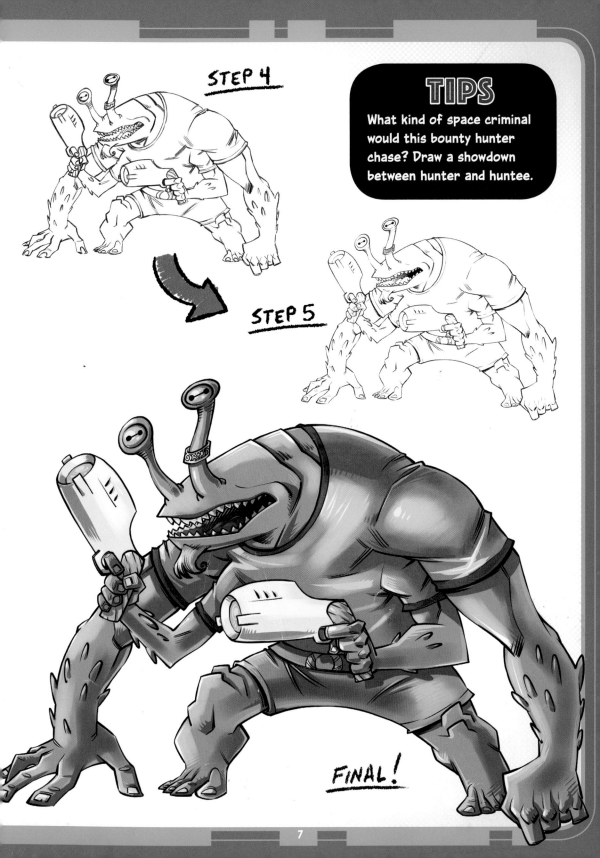

STEP 4

TIPS

What kind of space criminal would this bounty hunter chase? Draw a showdown between hunter and huntee.

STEP 5

FINAL!

QUEST FOR GOLD

Sail the high seas on a quest for gold – liquid gold, that is. This captain must collect all the honey he can, because even pirate bears have to hibernate in the winter.

STEP 1

STEP 2

STEP 3

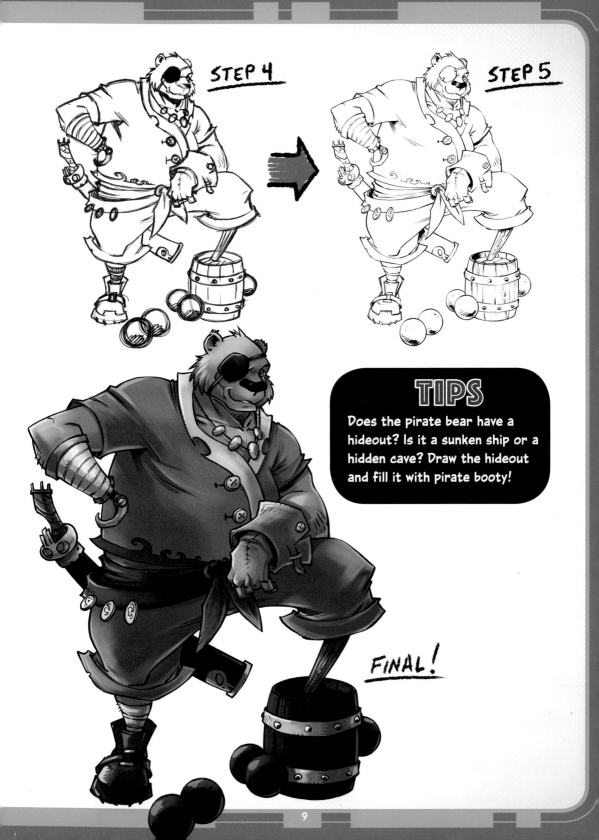

STEP 4

STEP 5

TIPS

Does the pirate bear have a hideout? Is it a sunken ship or a hidden cave? Draw the hideout and fill it with pirate booty!

FINAL!

BULL FIGHTER

Bull fighting takes on a whole new meaning when the bull is armed. Grab the bull by the horns – before he grabs you first!

STEP 1

STEP 2

STEP 3

STEP 4

STEP 5

FINAL!

TIPS

What do you think this bull is guarding? Draw a pile of treasure, a priceless gem or artifact, or even an unlucky prisoner.

MARTIAL ARTS MOUSE

Cats beware – there's a martial arts mouse on the loose! A well-placed smack on the nose with a nunchuck will make even the toughest tomcats back off.

STEP 1

STEP 2

STEP 3

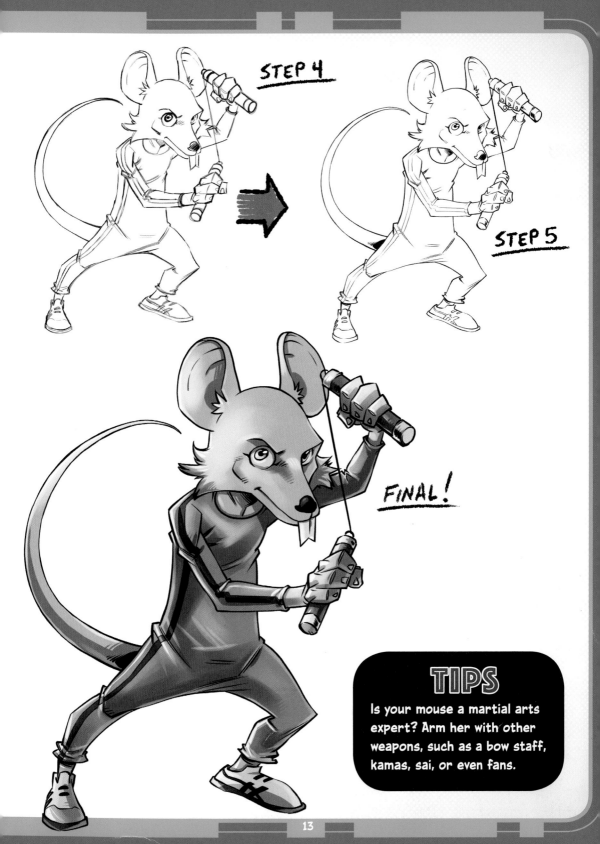

STEP 4

STEP 5

FINAL!

TIPS

Is your mouse a martial arts expert? Arm her with other weapons, such as a bow staff, kamas, sai, or even fans.

SLICE AND DICE

Kitchen assistants are a thing of the past when the chef has eight tentacles to get the job done. Just don't order the squid salad!

STEP 1

STEP 2

STEP 3

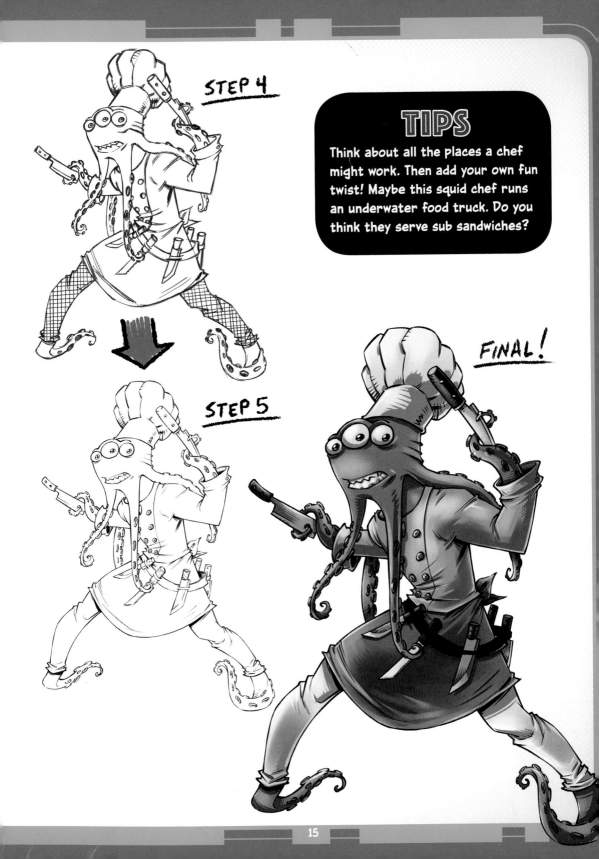

STEP 4

TIPS

Think about all the places a chef might work. Then add your own fun twist! Maybe this squid chef runs an underwater food truck. Do you think they serve sub sandwiches?

FINAL!

STEP 5

CHICKEN LITTLE JOHN

This Knight of the Egg-Shaped Table is ready for a quest! He robs from the rich, gives to the poor, and does his heroic best to keep the sky from falling.

STEP 1

STEP 2

STEP 3

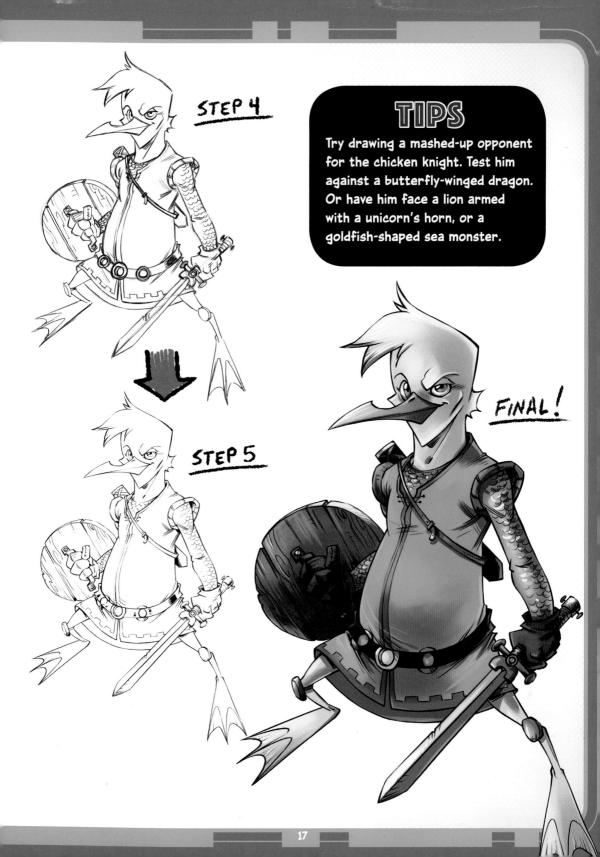

STEP 4

TIPS

Try drawing a mashed-up opponent for the chicken knight. Test him against a butterfly-winged dragon. Or have him face a lion armed with a unicorn's horn, or a goldfish-shaped sea monster.

FINAL!

STEP 5

A PURR IN THE DARK

Female ninja are called kunoichi. Would this warrior be a cat-noichi? Her stealthy skills send her on secret missions. They'll require a cat's patience and good ninjutsu – or should we say, ninjuts-mew?

STEP 1

STEP 2

STEP 3

STEP 4

STEP 5

FINAL!

TIPS

What is the ninja cat's mission? Is she attacking someone? Maybe she's guarding a VIP. Sketch who you think it might be.

NOT THE SHARPEST ARROW

Trolls may not be the smartest, but this one is the best with a bow! He can hit targets smaller than his own brain with ease. Fear him on the battlefield – just don't ask him any hard questions.

STEP 1

STEP 2

STEP 3

STEP 4

STEP 5

FINAL!

TIPS

Armor is important when you're going into a fight. Get creative and design the archer an entire suit.

ROCK 'N' ROLL

Go on, tell her she fights like a girl – I dare you! This rocker is a hard hitter and doesn't let anything slow her down.

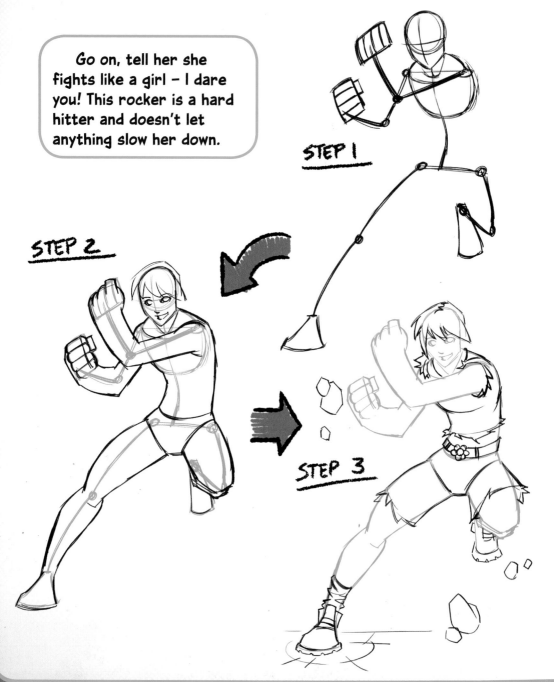

STEP 1

STEP 2

STEP 3

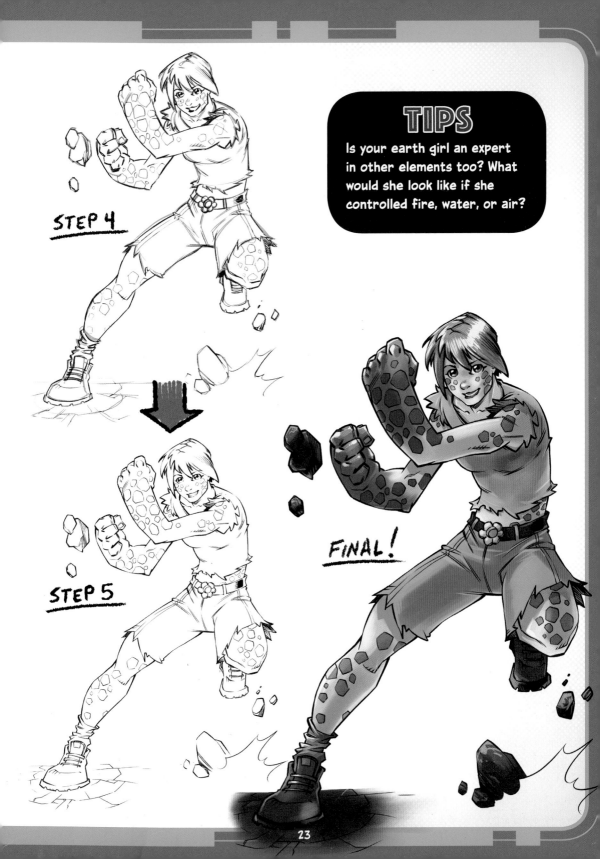

STEP 4

TIPS

Is your earth girl an expert in other elements too? What would she look like if she controlled fire, water, or air?

STEP 5

FINAL!

KILLER KARATE SQUASH

This karate master will squash any and all opponents. Get ready to be fruit-punched and kicked up!

STEP 1

STEP 2

STEP 3

STEP 4

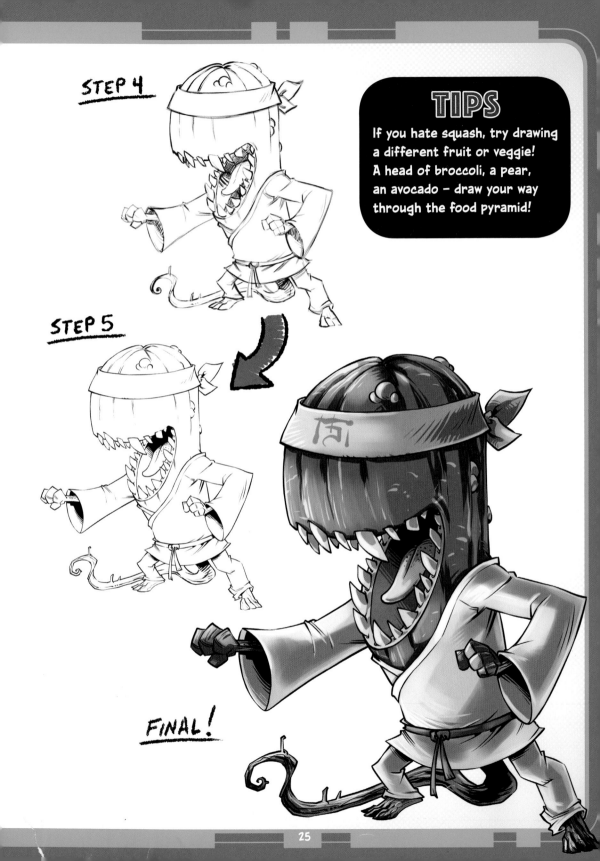

TIPS

If you hate squash, try drawing
a different fruit or veggie!
A head of broccoli, a pear,
an avocado – draw your way
through the food pyramid!

STEP 5

FINAL!

YIPPEE KI-YI-YOTE

The west was won by scrappy outlaws, and this cattle-rustlin' coyote cowboy is no exception. Will he be able to steer clear of the law? Or will he end up behind bars?

STEP 1

STEP 2

STEP 3

STEP 4

STEP 5

DEAD OR ALIVE

TNT

FINAL!

TIPS

Draw the old west town where your cowboy coyote is hiding. Is he hanging out in an old-fashioned saloon, or getting ready to hold up a bank?

DEAD OR ALIVE

TNT

SAMUROAR!

Sharp teeth and claws weren't enough for this warrior. The samurai dinosaur is armed with razor-sharp swords and throwing stars, too. T-rex better watch out!

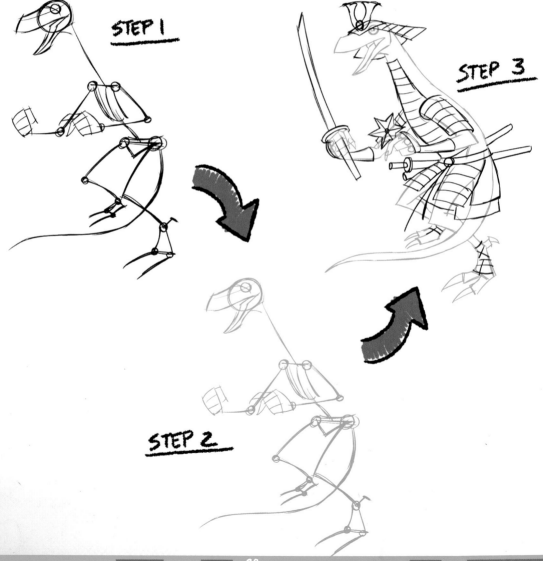

STEP 1

STEP 2

STEP 3

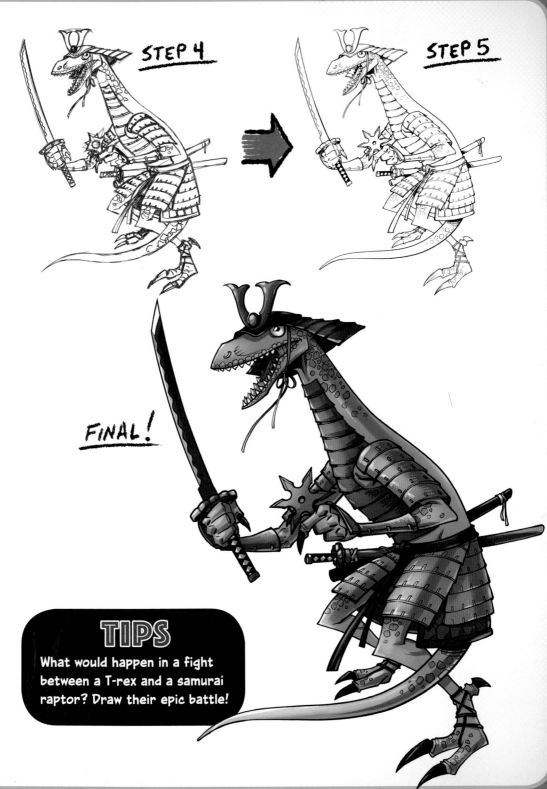

STEP 4

STEP 5

FINAL!

TIPS

What would happen in a fight between a T-rex and a samurai raptor? Draw their epic battle!

DRAGON DUDE

Dragons may live among us – but not in the way you might think. He can't fly, but this dragon-man mash-up has plenty of other fantastic features.

STEP 1

STEP 2

STEP 3

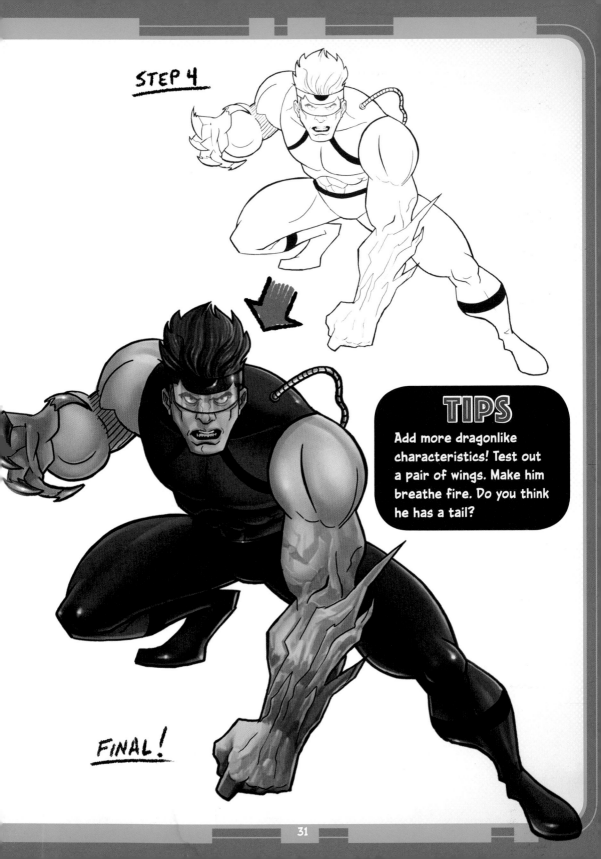

STEP 4

TIPS

Add more dragonlike characteristics! Test out a pair of wings. Make him breathe fire. Do you think he has a tail?

FINAL!

READ MORE

Gowen, Fiona. *How to Draw Scary Monsters and Other Mythical Creatures.* Hauppauge, N.Y.: Barrons Educational Series, 2017.

LaPadula, Tom. *Learn to Draw Military Machines: Step-by-Step Instructions for More Than 25 High-Powered Vehicles.* Lake Forest, Calif.: Walter Foster Publishing, 2016.

Sautter, Aaron. *How to Draw Orcs, Goblins, and Other Wicked Creatures.* North Mankato, Minn.: Capstone Press, 2016.

INTERNET SITES

Use FactHound to find Internet sites related to this book.

Visit *www.facthound.com*

Just type in 9781515769378 and go.

Check out projects, games and lots more at
www.capstonekids.com